Presented to

Hannah

By

Date

The Little Angel's
Bible Stories

The Little Angel's Bible Stories
Copyright © 1994 by Educational Publishing Concepts, Inc., Wheaton IL
Exclusive Distribution by Chariot Books

Published in Elgin, Illinois

ISBN 0-7814-0185-2

Printed in the United States of America
1 2 3 4 5 6 7 – 00 99 98 97 96 95 94

The Little Angel's
Bible Stories

Carolyn Larsen

Illustrated by
Rick Incrocci

Chariot Books ™
David C. Cook Publishing Co.

Dedication

To Cori, Mallory, and Ryan
my "little angels"
who helped give Ariana her personality.

CONTENTS

INSTRUCTION

PROTECTION

COMFORT

Announcements

DINNER FOR THREE

GENESIS 18:1-15

Ariana Angel wanted more than anything to serve God, the Father. For a long time Ariana had watched as the Father sent angels to care for His children on earth. She knew that He truly loved all people and that He even sent the Holy Spirit to live inside believers and help them. But sometimes He asked angels to help people by making announcements, teaching, protecting, and comforting.

Every time Ariana heard that the Father was asking for an angel helper she stood in line, but each time someone else was chosen. Ariana did not give up easily. In fact, she decided that some extra coaching might help. So she began a friendship with Michael, the dispatch angel. Michael was very glad to help the

young angel. He liked her eagerness and enthusiasm.

So this afternoon Ariana had arranged a meeting in the park with the older angel. Now she waited on a big rock in the shallow part of Lake Shalom. Her shoes and socks carelessly thrown on the ground, Ariana's feet dangled in the icy cold water.

"Ariana! Ariana! Where are you?" Michael called from the bridge.

"Coming, Sir," cried Ariana. She quickly slid off the rock and ran for shore. But before she knew what was happening, Ariana's foot slipped and she splashed headfirst into the cold water.

As she dragged her wet body out of the lake, she stammered through chattering teeth, "H-H-H-ere I-I-I am, Sir."

"Child, what happened to you?" Michael asked.

"Well, I, uh, sort of fell into the lake." Ariana was embarrassed. This was not the way to make a good impression.

"I see," Michael said, turning his head so she wouldn't see his smile. "Try to be a bit more careful. Now, what did you want to talk to me about?"

Ariana squeezed the water out of her little ponytail and straightened her hairband before speaking. Then she looked seriously at Michael. "Mr. Michael, I think I am ready to work in the Father's service. But every time He calls for an angel helper someone else is chosen. I was hoping you would tell me what to do so I can be ready the next time the Father has a job."

"I would be happy to teach you about our work for the Father. But you must realize that He chooses the angel helpers. I may make suggestions, but the decision is up to Him." Ariana nodded that she understood, so Michael continued. "Let's begin with the job of making announcements. When God has some special news for one of His people, He may ask one of us to deliver it."

16

"I can do that! I can! Just listen." Ariana opened her mouth as wide as she could and took a big breath.

"Wait, Ariana. Making announcements for the Father takes more than a loud voice. You must be sure you have all the facts straight, and that you tell the right person, and that... well, let me give you an example.

"A man named Abraham and his wife Sarah had wanted a child for a long, long time. In fact, God told them that someday they would have a huge family. But they grew very old and still did not have even one child. It seemed impossible that Sarah could have a baby at her age."

"Why did the Father promise something and then not do it?" Ariana was confused.

"You have not heard the

whole story yet," Michael reminded her. "One hot day Abraham was sitting at the door of his tent when three men walked up. Abraham politely offered them cool water to wash their feet. He asked them to sit in the shade of a tree near his home. He even told Sarah to quickly bake some bread for them. He chose one of his best young calves to be cooked. Then he brought that and the bread and some milk for the men to eat."

"My, he certainly did a lot of nice things for these men. Either Abraham didn't get much company, or he thought these men were pretty

special," Ariana observed.

Michael ignored her comment. "While they were eating, one of the men said, "I will come back to visit you about this time next year. By then Sarah will have a baby.""

"The angels! Those three visitors were angels, right?" Ariana was proud of herself for figuring this out.

"Right. Now when Sarah heard what the angel said she laughed right out loud!"

"Laughed? How rude! Didn't Sarah know that the Father can do anything

He wants to do?"

"Of course she knew that, but sometimes God's people get discouraged, and they forget how powerful God is. They forget how much He loves them. Even Abraham wondered if the angel knew what he was talking

about. But of course he did. He had the facts straight and he had delivered them to the right people. Sure enough, a year later Abraham and Sarah had a son."

"You know, this announcement business sounds pretty good. I mean, those three angels got a nice meal, made a simple announcement, and the job was done," Ariana said.

"Well, there was a bit more to it than that. Now Ariana, you better run home and put on dry clothes. You're dripping on my robe."

"Oooops. Sorry. OK I'll go, but I'll come back later for more stories," Ariana said as she picked up her shoes and socks.

"I am certain you will," Michael said. "I am certain you will."

Thinking It Over

• What did Ariana want to do?
• How would you like to serve God?

THE BIGGEST ANNOUNCEMENT EVER

LUKE 1:26-38

"Hear Ye. Hear Ye—all the Father's children!" Ariana shouted at the top of her lungs.

"What's all the racket?" Michael called, leaning out his office window.

"O, it's just me, Mr. Michael," Ariana said. "I'm practicing making announcements so I can be an announcer angel."

"Ariana, come up here. We need to talk."

"Yes, Sir," Ariana said. Then

turning to her imaginary audience, she shouted, "There will be no more announcements at this time."

When the little angel came into his office, Michael motioned for her to sit down.

"I'm going to keep practicing so I'll be ready to make the biggest announcement the Father ever needs made!" Ariana said.

"I'm glad you are so eager to serve. But I think God's biggest announcement has already been made," Michael said. Ariana looked so disappointed that Michael quickly asked, "Would you like to hear about it?" The little angel nodded so he continued. "This big news was

announced by the Angel Gabriel."

"Oh, I've heard of him. He's the most important of all the Father's angels!" Ariana said without thinking. "Uhhh, I mean, except for you, of course. Gabriel is really the *second* most important."

Michael smiled as he continued.

"The important announcement the Father gave him to make was to a young girl named Mary. She was a sweet, young girl, engaged to marry a man named Joseph."

"What could God want to tell a young girl?" Ariana wondered aloud. "Doesn't He only care about grown-ups?"

"The Father cares for all His children, young or old. Mary loved God and always tried to live in a way that would please Him. God was very happy with Mary. That's why He chose her to receive this special announcement."

"What was it? What did Gabriel say to Mary?"

"He said, 'Mary, the Lord is very happy with you. He sent me to tell you that you are going to have a baby. He will be a very special baby. He will be the Son of God, and you will name Him Jesus.'"

"The Son of God? Wow! Mary must have been soooooo excited! I sure understand why Gabriel got to make this announcement."

"Yes. This announcement was worthy of the best announcer the Father had. And yes, Mary was excited. Except that because she wasn't married, she didn't really understand how she could have a baby. But Gabriel reminded her that

anything is possible with God."

"That was really a happy announcement. But, Mr. Michael, why do you say that was the Father's biggest announcement ever?"

"Because, Little One, it was an important part of God's plan of salvation for all people. The birth of this baby had been predicted for hundreds of years. Because Jesus came to earth as a baby then, any person can now become a member of God's family. Of course, there was more to the plan, Jesus also died on a cross

for the sins of all people. Then He rose from the dead and now is here in heaven with His Father."

"Gabriel's announcement *was* part of something really big!" Ariana said. Then she slumped in her chair, completely discouraged.

"Ariana, what's the matter?"

Michael asked.

"I wanted to make the Father's biggest announcement," Ariana mumbled. "If it has already been made, then there's no use even practicing anymore."

"Don't let your pride get in the way, Little One. We can each serve God by doing whatever He asks us to do. Anything He wants done is important." Michael gently explained.

"I suppose you're right," she said, her spirit returning. "OK, I'll go practice some more. See ya later!"

"I am certain you will," Michael said. "I am certain you will."

Thinking It Over

• What was "the biggest announcement ever"?
• Thank God for His plan of salvation. Thank Jesus for coming to earth for you.

THE BRIGHT SKY

LUKE 2:8-20

"**M**r. Michael, Mr. Michael, are you up?" The shrill voice combined with the pounding on his door rang through the early morning darkness. Michael struggled to his feet and pulled on his robe, then stumbled to the door.

"Ariana, is that you? Why are you knocking on my door so early?" Michael was gentle, as always. That was a lesson in itself for the little angel.

"Mr. Michael, I have a question about that announcement Gabriel gave to Mary."

"All right. Come in Ariana," Michael

sighed. He turned on a light in the living room and sat down in his favorite chair. "Now, what's your question?"

Ariana tossed some pillows from the sofa on the floor and stretched out on her tummy. One foot bounced in the air as she spoke. "Well, I was thinking that if the baby Mary was going to have was part of God's plan to save the whole world, then someone must have made an announcement to the whole world. Did Gabriel get to give that news, too?"

"So you have been thinking about my story, eh?" Michael said. "Yes. The Father did arrange for an announcement to be made to the world. But, no, Gabriel didn't give it. As a matter of fact, a—"

"You mean a regular angel got to announce that the Son of God was born?" Ariana jumped to her feet. "That is so neat...did he get to go to palaces and give the news to kings and queens? I would love to see palaces. They must be so beautiful. The baby was born in one, right?" Ariana was completely starry-eyed.

"Slow down, Ariana. Let me tell you what actually happened." Michael took a minute to stretch before he began. "You might expect that the Son of God would be born in a palace, surrounded by the finest things of the world. But the Father wanted to be sure that everyone knew that Jesus came to be the Savior of all people. He wasn't born just for rich people or royalty. So the special baby was not born in a palace, He was born in a stable."

"A what?"

"A stable, you know, where farm

animals live," Michael explained patiently.

"Animals? The Savior of the world was born in a barn? You must have your stories mixed up, Mr. Michael. I can't believe the Son of God would be born in a place like that. Why, have you ever smelled a—"

Michael interrupted quickly,

"Ariana, you are missing the point. Jesus was born as a common everyday person so that common everyday people would know Him. If He had been born in a palace, only royalty would have known Him. Anyway, let's get back to the announcement part of the story. After the baby was born, the Father wanted everyone to know. So, He sent an angel to make the announcement. But, it wasn't made in a fancy palace to kings. It was made on a quiet hillside to shepherds who were caring for their sheep."

Ariana was totally confused now.

"It happened on a dark, quiet night. The shepherds were out on a hillside watching their sheep. Suddenly the sky became as light as daytime. That was the angel lighting up the sky. You can imagine how scared the shepherds were. But the angel told them not to be afraid. Then he announced to them, 'I have great news for all of you. A baby was born tonight in Bethlehem. His name is Jesus and He will save the whole world from sin.' "

"Wow. One angel got to tell the whole world!" Ariana mumbled.

"Well, one made the announcement, but then a whole choir of angels joined him. They all praised God together. Then they disappeared as quickly as they came. The shepherds were so excited that they hurried to Bethlehem to see the new baby."

"That story is nothing like I expected. Are you sure He was born in a stable?" Ariana asked softly.

"I'm sure," Michael said gently.

"I need to think about this," Ariana said. "I'll be back later, Sir."

"I am certain you will," Michael yawned. "I am certain you will."

Thinking It Over

• Whom did the angel tell about Jesus' birth?
• Whom can you tell about Jesus?

THE FIRST SIGN LANGUAGE

LUKE 1:5-25; 57-66

"Jesus loves you this I know," Ariana sang softly. She sat near a quiet stream, gently rocking the baby doll in her arms.

"Hello, Ariana. What a cute doll. What is her name?" Michael asked.

"Oh hello, Mr. Michael. Angela, this is Mr. Michael. Mr. Michael, this is Angela," Ariana said as she laid the doll down in her cradle.

"Mr. Michael, I really liked your story about angels announcing the birth of Jesus. I think I would like to make those kinds of announcements. Are there any more angel stories about baby announcements?"

"Yes. There are several more stories. Would you like to hear one?" Michael asked.

"Yes, please. But not too loudly. Angela needs to nap for a while," Ariana whispered.

"Oh, certainly," Michael agreed, moving a few feet away. He sat down on an old tree stump and began, "Well, Zechariah is another person who received an angel announcement. It was about the birth of his son. Zechariah was a priest so he worked at the temple. The day the angel came to him he was alone in the inner part of the temple. Only the priests could go in

this special place. Many people were outside waiting for Zechariah. They had to wait for a long time, and they didn't know what was going on inside.

"Zechariah was lighting incense, which was part of his job, when all of a sudden there was an angel standing next to him. By the way, it so happens that this announcement was also made by Gabriel."

"He gets all the really important jobs," Ariana admitted.

"*Any* job we are asked to do for the Father is important," Michael reminded her.

"Anyway, Zechariah was busily doing his job when the angel Gabriel suddenly appeared. Of course, Zechariah was afraid. I mean, it wasn't every day that an angel came to see him. But Gabriel was gentle. He said, 'God has heard the prayers of you and your wife about having a baby. I am here to tell you that your wife Elizabeth will have a son and you shall name him John.' "

"How come Zechariah and Elizabeth didn't get to name their own baby? Isn't that part of the fun of having a baby?"

"Zechariah and Elizabeth were happy to do whatever God said. They had waited a long time for a baby. But the interesting thing is that they were both very old, so Zechariah didn't really believe that they could become parents now."

"Just like Abraham and Sarah, huh? Remember how Sarah laughed when the angel said she would have a baby? She thought she was too old," Ariana explained.

"That's right. But this time, Gabriel said, 'I came to tell you the good news that God is giving you a child. But because you did not believe, you will not be able to speak until the baby is born.'"

"Not be able to talk? Oh, that would be terrible!" Ariana's voice trembled at the very thought.

"Well, that would be bad for you, wouldn't it? When Zechariah came out of the temple, all the people were waiting for him. They wanted to know why he had been inside so long. But he couldn't tell them. They finally figured out from the signs he made that he had seen an angel. Of course, they didn't know what the angel said to him."

"Was that the first time sign language was used?" Ariana asked.

"Could be. Anyway, Zechariah wasn't able to say a word until his wife Elizabeth gave birth to a baby boy. Actually, he couldn't speak until

he wrote down that the baby was to be named John. None of their neighbors or relatives could understand that choice. They thought the baby should be named after Zechariah. But the parents followed the angel's directions and right away Zechariah got his voice back."

"That's a great story. Mr. Angel Gabriel does a good job, doesn't he?

"Oh dear, Angela is waking up," Ariana picked up her baby. "You know, I think I'll teach her some sign language. It sounds like that might be a good thing to know. Angela and I will make a great team someday."

"I am certain you will," Michael said. "I am certain you will."

Thinking It Over

• Why did Zechariah lose his voice?
• Like Zechariah, thank God for your prayers that He has answered.

GET OUT OF TOWN!

MATTHEW 2:13, 19-21

"So Ariana, do you think you would like to make baby announcements for the Father?" Michael asked as the little angel swung higher and higher.

When the swing was at it's highest point, Ariana jumped out, and landed in the soft grass below.

"I don't think that was a very safe thing to do, Little One. And it certainly was not very angel-like," Michael scolded.

"Sorry." Ariana smoothed her robe and straightened her belt. "I was thinking about the baby announcements." It seemed like a good idea to change the subject. "It certainly is good news when a baby is coming. I would like bringing good news to people. But, I think I would like something a little more, um, you know—exciting." Ariana's big dark eyes opened wide. "Something adventurous or even dangerous. Are there any angel announcement stories like that?"

"Yes. There certainly are. In fact, one exciting announcement was about baby Jesus."

"You mean Mary's baby? What could be dangerous about Him? He was God's Son, so wasn't He sort of protected?"

"Yes. He was protected. In fact, that's what the story is about. The Father asked for an angel to play a

43

big part in His protection." Michael definitely had Ariana's attention now, so he continued. "When little Jesus was born, King Herod was very jealous. Everyone was talking about this new king who had been born. Herod was afraid that Jesus would take his kingdom away from him."

"That's silly. Jesus wasn't that kind of king, was He?"

"No, but King Herod didn't know that, and he didn't want to take any chances that a new king might take over, so he did something terrible. He knew that Jesus was in Bethlehem, but he didn't know which baby He was. So Herod ordered his soldiers to kill all the baby boys in Bethlehem."

"That's awful. The mothers and fathers must have been so afraid.

Why, I just wouldn't let them do that. I would fight and scream and—" Ariana was shadowboxing all around Michael.

"Ariana, calm down. The Father knew what was happening. He sent an angel to take an emergency message to Joseph."

"What did the angel do? Stand guard in front of their house?"

"No. The angel messenger went to see Joseph while he was sleeping. He appeared to him in a dream and told him that a bad king wanted to kill Jesus. He told Joseph to take Jesus and Mary out

45

of the country."

"Did Joseph do it?" Ariana asked.

"Of course. The little family left for Egypt right away."

"They must have left everything they owned behind. That would be hard to do. Did they ever come back home?"

"Yes. A few years later King Herod died. Then the Father sent an angel to tell Joseph that it was safe to return home."

"Well, that is definitely more exciting than a baby announcement. I would like to deliver those kinds of

messages for the Father. It's almost like being a secret agent. I'm gonna be the best secret agent angel ever!" Ariana announced.

Michael smiled, "I am certain you will," he said. "I am certain you will."

Thinking It Over

• Why did Joseph have to get Jesus out of the country?

• Thank God for protecting baby Jesus. Thank Him for taking care of you, too!

A TERRIBLE STORM

Acts 23:12-15; 27:13-44

Michael and Ariana were walking down a peaceful street, side by side. Ariana's usual perky chatter was missing today. "Ariana, I have never seen you so quiet. Are you all right?" There was true concern in Michael's voice.

"Yes, Sir. I'm fine. No. I'm not. Mr. Michael, Sir, is there anything you are afraid of?" Ariana asked earnestly.

"Afraid? Hmm. No, I can't say that there is. Why do you ask?"

" 'Cause I was reading this book last night and it was about a terrible storm with lightning flashing and thunder crashing and rain pounding and wind blowing and..."

"Stop and take a breath, Ariana. Why does this story of a storm scare you so much? We don't have storms in heaven. You will never have to see lightning or hear thunder—Uh oh!" Michael stopped suddenly.

"What? What's the matter? You know something. Tell me," Ariana cried.

"It's just that I suddenly remembered a time when an angel

helping the Father had to deliver a message to someone right in the middle of a terrible storm."

"It wasn't the storm to end all storms—when the whole world was destroyed—was it?" Ariana asked, remembering Noah.

"Oh, no. It was nothing like that storm. Although it was pretty powerful. Can I tell you about it?"

Ariana looked doubtful. "Well, OK. But hurry through the storm part."

"The story centers around Paul. You may remember some stories about him. He once hated everyone who followed Jesus, but after Paul became a Christian, he spent his whole life telling people about God."

"Yeah, and he got in trouble for it sometimes, too," the little angel recalled.

"That's exactly right. In fact, in this story Paul had been teaching and

50

preaching and making religious leaders angry again. He was arrested and put in jail in Jerusalem. But they had to move him to a different prison because—"

"A terrible storm ripped the roof right off the buildings and the Romans were afraid Paul would escape." Ariana was pretty sure she had this right.

"No, he was moved because some people were so angry at him, that they might break into the prison and kill him."

"You hardly ever hear of people trying to break into prison!" Ariana laughed.

"Well, that's what they were going to try to do. So partly because of the threats, and partly because Paul was a Roman citizen, he was put on a boat that was sailing for Rome. When he

got there Caesar would hear his case. But in the middle of the trip to Rome a big storm blew up on the sea."

"I have a bad feeling about this," Ariana said nervously.

"The sailors fought to keep their ship on course, but the winds of the storm were too strong. They finally gave in and let the ship go with the wind. But, the storm seemed to grow more and more powerful.

"They threw the cargo of the ship over into the sea to keep the ship light enough to float. Dark clouds filled the sky so that they couldn't even see the sun or stars for many days. The storm went on so long that the sailors gave up hope. They even stopped eating. They were sure they were all going to die.

"But then, in the middle of the night God sent an angel to see Paul."

"Right in the middle of the storm? An angel had to be there with the wind and thunder and lightning on a boat in the middle of the sea?" Ariana whispered.

"That's right. An angel took this message from God to Paul. He told Paul not to be afraid because he was going to make it to Rome to stand trial before Caesar. He also told Paul that no one on the ship would die in the storm. So Paul told all the sailors to be brave because he trusted God to keep His word."

"Paul was just a prisoner on the ship. And he told everyone else to be brave?"

"Yes. Paul was an example to

everyone else of a man who trusted in God."

"So, was the angel right? Were they all safe?"

"Yes. They were safe, but they did have a shipwreck. That is another story. Paul did eventually make it to Rome. Anyway, it is possible that in the Father's service you may have to experience a thunderstorm. You will just have to trust Him to keep you safe."

"I guess you're right. But, just in case, I'm going to read up on storm safety. I want you to be safe, too, so I'll come and explain it all to you," Ariana said as she ran down the street.

"I am certain you will," Michael said. "I am certain you will."

Thinking It Over

- Why was Paul going to Rome?
- What are you afraid of?
- How can God help you not be so afraid?

Instruction

YOU CAN DO IT!

JUDGES 6:11-22

Michael settled down in a hammock between two enormous oak trees. He watched two squirrels playing high up in the branches before he opened a book. He was enjoying this break from his busy day, but the peacefulness didn't last long. "Mr. Michael, I have an idea," Ariana rushed up so quickly that Michael's hammock rocked high up in the air.

He grabbed the sides and held on. When it stopped swinging he laid down his book and struggled out. Smoothing his robes, he asked, "What is your idea, Little One?"

"Well, I was just thinking about things I am good at. I'm really good at talking and telling people what to do. So I was thinking that maybe that's the kind of job I could do for the Father. What do you think, Mr. Michael, could God use a talent for talking, huh?" Ariana rambled.

Michael thought for a moment before answering. "Yes. I do know of several times when the Father asked for an angel to give some direction to one of His people. One time an angel had to convince a man that there was a job he could do for God."

"I'm really good at convincing. I can talk my friends into doing almost

anything… " Ariana realized too late that this might not be good information to give the other angel. "Anyway," she continued quickly, "I think I could do that job."

Michael shook his head, "Listen to the story, Ariana. This angel appeared to Gideon because the nation of Israel was being bullied by the Midianites. The Israelites cried out to God to help them. The Father always helps when His people ask Him. So, God sent an angel to tell Gideon that God was with the Israelites. Gideon was a little confused by this news. If God was with the Israelites, why had so many terrible things happened to them? He had heard stories of how God had done miracles for His people in the past,

but the Midianites had been picking on Gideon and his people for so long that he thought God had left them."

"Sounds as if Gideon was discouraged. That angel must have had to do a lot of talking to get Gideon moving. Yep, that's a job for me," the little angel said confidently.

"This angel assured Gideon that the Lord would help him save the Israelites. They would work together to strike down all the Midianites. Gideon still wasn't sure so he asked the angel to give him a sign that God would really be with him."

"What did he want, writing in the sky?"

"Just listen, please. The angel waited while Gideon prepared some meat and bread as an offering to God. When Gideon brought them out, the angel said, 'Just put them on that rock there.' Gideon did and the angel touched the tip of his staff to them. Fire came shooting out and burned up the meat and bread. Then the angel disappeared."

"Awesome! How did he do that?" Ariana picked up a stick and started touching everything around her.

"Gideon knew now that the Lord really would be with him so he could begin fighting the Midianites."

"I can do a job like that. I can!" Ariana insisted. "I just gotta learn the fire part. How do I learn that?"

"God did that part, Ariana. When

He sends us to do a job, He gives us whatever help we need."

"Well, I'm going to practice. Maybe the Father will help me cook something," Ariana insisted. "Practice makes perfect, you know! I will see you later, Sir."

"I am certain you will," Michael sighed. "I am certain you will."

Thinking It Over

• Who did the Israelites need help defeating?
• What problem would you like God to help you with? Ask Him to help.

WHICH WAY DO I GO?

ACTS 8:5-8, 26-40

"**M**ary Ellen, please take our attendance sheet to the office. Tommy, please write all the spelling words on the board. All right class, open your spelling books to page forty-seven," Ariana instructed her class.

"You are very good at giving instructions," Michael said as he came into her classroom. "Your students are very well behaved too," he said, looking over the rows of stuffed bunnies, teddy bears, and pretty little dolls.

"Well, I have a lot of experience," Ariana said importantly. "Students can tell when a teacher knows what she is talking about, you know."

"Being able to give good, clear instructions can be a very helpful skill in the Father's service. Even when someone is already serving God and telling others about His love, he may need further instruction and guidance."

"If someone is already doing what the Father wants, why does he need more instruction?" Ariana didn't understand this line of thinking.

"Well, for example, there was once a

man named Philip. The Father sent Philip to another land, called Samaria, to tell the people there about God's love and that Jesus died for them. Philip was doing a wonderful job of telling everyone about God. Many people believed in Him."

"Sounds like everything was going just as God would want. What's the problem?" Ariana asked. She began stacking up her school books.

"The problem, Little One, was that there was another man, in another place who was beginning to read the Scriptures and wonder about God. But he couldn't understand the Scriptures unless someone explained them to him."

"So why didn't he go to a church or temple and ask someone?" The

answer to his problem seemed simple to Ariana.

"He could have done that, I suppose. But the Father had a better idea. He asked an angel to visit Philip. The angel told Philip to leave his work in Samaria and go south to the desert road that goes from Jerusalem to Gaza. Philip didn't even ask why; he just did what the angel said. And on that road, he met the man who was wondering about God. Philip explained how Jesus had come and died for his sins; and how God loved the man. They stopped and right there in some water by the road, Philip baptized the man."

"The man became a believer because the angel sent Philip? That angel must have been very happy!"

"Yes! He was very happy to have been a part of the plan. But you see the angel gave very clear instructions. That's how Philip knew where to go."

"Class, put away your spelling books now. Take out your geography books. We are going to study maps for the rest of the day," Ariana suddenly announced. Then she turned back to Michael, "I am going to study maps with the class. Then I can give directions to anywhere. I'll come show you!"

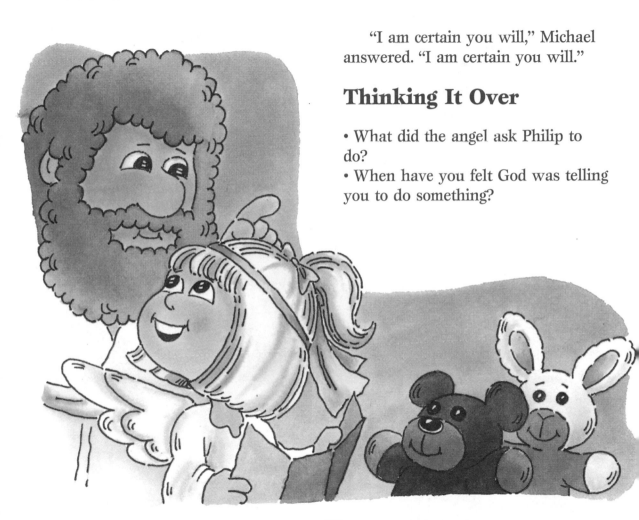

"I am certain you will," Michael answered. "I am certain you will."

Thinking It Over

• What did the angel ask Philip to do?
• When have you felt God was telling you to do something?

FOLLOWING GOD'S DIRECTIONS

ACTS 10:3-8, 30-32

The door to Michael's office burst open and Ariana ran in. "Mr. Michael, I have the maps memorized. Ask me where anyplace is and I can tell you. Go ahead, ask me anything. The only thing I still have a little trouble with is which way is east and which way is west. But, I'm working on it."

Michael put aside his paperwork and smiled at the eager, young angel.

"I'm proud of you, Ariana. You have been working very hard. I can see that you are very serious about serving the Father."

"I am, Sir. I really am. Has He called for any direction-giving jobs lately?"

"Well, I haven't heard of any recently. But I can tell you about one other time an angel gave directions. Would you like to hear?"

"Sure," Ariana said. She laid her maps down and ran to get a pillow from the couch before settling down on the floor.

"This story is about a man

named Cornelius," Michael began. "He was a Gentile man."

"A *gentle* man?"

"No, a *Gentile*. That was a person who wasn't part of the Jewish nation or religion. Gentiles believed different things than the Jews did. The Jews and the Gentiles did not have much to do with each other. But Cornelius knew God and he prayed every day and gave money to the poor—"

"But, he hadn't studied maps so he needed directions to someplace," Ariana interrupted impatiently.

"No. That's not it. One day Cornelius had a vision—"

"What's a vision?"

"If you will stop interrupting, I will explain it to you," Michael said patiently. "A vision is kind of like a

dream that you have in the daytime. In this vision an angel came to Cornelius. The angel said, 'Send your men to Joppa to bring back a man named Peter. They will find him staying at Simon's house which is near the sea.'"

"There are the directions. They are so important. Just think if the men had to search all through Joppa for that man's house, and they didn't look by the sea until the very last. Whew!" Ariana was overwhelmed at the thought. "Why did the angel want Peter to come to Cornelius' house anyway?"

"Peter traveled around teaching and preaching about God. But, until

now he had only preached to Jewish people. He thought God only loved the Jews. He never thought about preaching to Gentiles. Now God was showing Peter that the Gentiles as well as the Jews needed to hear about God's love. Peter had a dream at about the same time as Cornelius' vision. The dream showed Peter that God wanted everyone of all nations to know Him. If Peter hadn't had the dream, he might not have gone to Cornelius' house. This was

part of God's plan to spread His message of love to the whole world."

"Wow. That is two times when an angel helped someone learn about God. I like this job. Tell you what, I'll be sitting right outside your door so I'll be first in line the next time the Father needs an angel who knows her directions. I'll be ready, Sir!"

"I am certain you will," Michael said. "I am certain you will."

Thinking It Over

• Why did Peter need a dream to tell him to visit Cornelius?
• Thank God for the person who told you about God's love.

Protection

PRISON BREAK

ACTS 12:1-13

*S*tomp! Stomp! Stomp! Even before he saw her blond head peek around his office door, Michael knew who was coming up the stairs. But, just in case there was any doubt, she announced herself loudly, "Mr. Michael, it's Ariana, Sir."

"Hello, Ariana. What can I do for you today?"

"I heard the Father needs someone for a job. I want to go, Mr.
Michael, I really do. I know I can do
it. Please give me a chance. I want to
serve the Father like the other angels.
Please, Sir." The words tumbled from
Ariana.

"Ariana, helping the Father care
for His children is serious work. You
are very young. There is still much
for you to learn." Michael was gentle,
but firm.

"What else do I need to learn? Tell me and I will learn it," begged Ariana.

"A part of our work that I haven't explained yet is protecting God's children, whom He loves very much. Let me give you an example.

"Peter was in prison. The Father's desire was to protect Peter. So He chose one of our brightest, quickest angels. One night when Peter was sleeping, the angel slipped into his cell and woke him. Such a bright light filled his prison cell that Peter could hardly see."

Michael smiled at the memory. "Then the angel said, 'Get up!' But Peter couldn't because he was chained between two guards. Without saying a word, the angel made the chains fall off Peter's wrists."

"Wow! How did he do that?" Ariana cried.

"Shh. Just listen! The most difficult job was still ahead. The protector angel had to get Peter out of prison quickly. Sixteen more guards were watching Peter, and none of them were planning to let him leave. Not only that, but all the doors were tightly locked."

"Oh my! They were trapped, weren't they? What could the angel possibly do?" Ariana wondered aloud.

"Ahhh, Ariana. This is where experience is necessary. The angel knew exactly what to ask the Father to do. He led Peter past the guards.

Not one guard tried to stop them! They did not even seem to see Peter and the angel walking by."

"But what about the locked doors? They couldn't just walk out," said Ariana.

"When the Father is helping, Little One, anything can happen. As

Peter and the angel came to them, the prison doors swung open, and they walked right out to the street. Then, before Peter could say a word, the angel left. His work was finished."

"What did Peter do then?" asked Ariana.

"Why, he hurried to see his friends. They were praying for his safety. He wanted them to know how the Father answered their prayers."

"How did Peter know that the angel was an angel?" Ariana asked.

"Good question. He didn't at first. In fact, he thought he was dreaming. It was really only after the angel left that Peter understood what had happened.

"So, Ariana, do you think you are ready to do the Father's work?"

"I guess not," Ariana mumbled. "I do have a bit more to learn." Then her mood brightened, "But I learn fast. I'll be back," she called as she dashed out the door.

"I am certain you will," Michael answered. "I am certain you will."

Thinking It Over

• When was a time that God protected you?
• Thank God for watching over you and protecting you.

A TALKING DONKEY

NUMBERS 22:1-35

Michael finished his evening prayers and was leaving the little chapel when Ariana ran up so quickly, she nearly knocked him down. "Mr. Michael, Mr. Michael, I can do it...am I ready now?" she shouted.

"What can you do, Ariana?" Michael asked kindly.

"I can shine! I can shine so brightly your eyes will hurt. Can I show you? Please, can I?"

"All right Ariana, let me see you shine," Michael said, sitting down on the bench near the chapel door.

Ariana closed her eyes and concentrated. As she did, her chubby cheeks began to puff out. She worked so hard that her face was soon bright red and her cheeks were as big as grapefruits. But, she was shining. "Very good, Ariana, I can see you have been practicing," Michael said, hiding a smile.

"So, am I ready? Can I serve the Father now?" Ariana asked.

"Ariana, I am glad you are so eager to serve, but there is more to doing the Father's work than shining. Sometimes shining is not even necessary. One time an angel was not even seen by the person he was helping."

Ariana sank down on the floor and looked puzzled.

"For this job, the angel was only seen by a donkey who was carrying—"

"A DONKEY? I thought we only helped God's CHILDREN. Why was this angel helping a donkey?" Ariana interrupted.

"Just listen, please. The donkey was taking a man named Balaam to see King Balak. The king was upset that the Israelites were in his country.

He wanted Balaam to put a curse on them."

"Didn't the king know how powerful God is and that He protects His children?" Ariana asked.

"As a matter of fact, that is exactly why he wanted them out of his land. He knew that other nations had been destroyed to protect God's children. His plan was for Balaam to put a curse on them, and then he would drive them out of the land."

"Did Balaam agree to do it?" Ariana asked.

"He asked the Father what he should do. The Father said, 'Don't do it.' But then the king offered Balaam money. Balaam asked God again if he

could go. The Father said, 'Yes. BUT you must only say what I tell you to say.' Early the next day Balaam packed his things on a donkey and left."

"Is this where the angel comes in?" Ariana asked eagerly.

"Yes. The angel had to stop Balaam from making a big mistake. So he stood in the middle of the road. The donkey saw him, but Balaam did not. When the donkey left the road to get away from the angel, Balaam got mad and hit her."

"Ooooo. That's not nice. He shouldn't have hit the donkey," Ariana said loudly.

"The donkey went back on the road, but there was the angel again. This time, the donkey squeezed next to a wall. Maybe she was trying to get past the angel. But, Balaam's foot was crushed between the donkey and the wall. Now, he was even more angry! He beat the donkey again, harder than before."

"Poor donkey," Ariana mumbled.

"The donkey went back on the road again. And there was the angel, again, right in front of the donkey. This time there was no place for the

donkey to go. So she just lay down. Now Balaam was very angry. He beat the animal and shouted. That's when the Father let the donkey speak."

"A talking donkey? Neat! Did the donkey tell Balaam what she thought of him?"

"Ariana, please. The donkey simply asked, 'Why are you beating me?' She thought Balaam could see the angel, too. Balaam was too angry to even be surprised that his donkey was talking. He shouted, 'You are making a fool out of me. If I had a sword, I would kill you!' "

"Then God let Balaam see the angel standing there, with his sword drawn. The angel said, 'Why did you beat your donkey? If she had kept going, I would have killed you. Your donkey saved your life.'

"Balaam was amazed, 'I-I-I have sinned. I-I-I didn't see you. Should I go home?'

"'No. You may go to the king. But, only say what the Father tells you,' the angel said firmly. That, Ariana, is the story of an invisible angel."

"There is something I don't understand. The Father said Balaam could go, then He sent an angel to stop him. Did the Father change His mind?" Ariana asked.

"Good question. God did say Balaam could go. But the Father saw that Balaam was getting caught up in the money and honor the king offered. He was not strong enough to do what God wanted. So, to protect the Israelites, He had to stop Balaam."

"Ooohhh," Ariana moaned and fell back on the floor.

"Ariana, what's wrong?"

"Now I have to learn to be *invisible*. I thought I was ready." But soon, her energy returned and Ariana jumped to her feet. "I better start

91

practicing. I'll be back, Sir!" she shouted as she ran out the door.

"I am certain you will," Michael said, smiling. "I am certain you will!"

Thinking It Over

• Balaam started out obeying the Father. Where did his problems start?

• When was a time you got caught up in the honor of being praised by others? How did you get back on the right track?

HUNGRY LIONS

Daniel 6:1-23

Michael was enjoying an evening stroll through the quiet lawns, when he heard an unmistakable voice. "Ariana, is that you?" he called. No response. "Ariana, where are you?" he called, looking all around. Still no response, yet he was sure he had heard her voice again. Michael began to wonder if Ariana had mastered the art of becoming invisible. He knew she had been working on this difficult skill.

Suddenly Michael spotted a blond ponytail bouncing from behind a tree.

He walked over quietly. The littlest angel in all the angel brigade was sitting by the tree, her head propped unhappily on her hands. "Ariana, why so sad?" Michael asked gently.

"O, Mr. Michael, Sir, I keep trying to learn everything I need to know to serve the Father. But just when I think I'm ready, I find out there is something else I must learn," Ariana cried.

"Well, you don't have to learn everything at once, you know," Michael answered kindly.

"I know," Ariana admitted, but she wasn't ready to stop complaining.

"Becoming invisible is *hard*. I've been trying all day and I haven't been invisible once! I wish one of the angel job requirements was being good with animals," Ariana said. She held out some crumbs and a fluffy-tailed squirrel ate right out of her hand.

"Actually, I can think of one time when being good with animals was a big part of an angel's job," Michael said.

"Really? You aren't just trying to make me feel better?"

"Really. Here is what happened. A servant of the Father named Daniel was living in another country."

"Why?" Ariana asked.

"His whole nation had

been captured and taken to Babylon. The king of Babylon noticed that Daniel was smart and that he could be trusted. So he made Daniel a ruler of one part of the country."

"He turned a prisoner into a ruler? Did the other ruler people in Bab—Baba—did the other rulers like that?"

"Babylon. No, as a matter of fact, they were jealous of Daniel. They thought the king liked him too much and that he had too much power. So they looked for some way to get Daniel in trouble. But, he was so honest and such a hard worker, that there was nothing bad about him to tell the king."

"Hah! Guess they found out that God's people are the best!" Ariana gloated.

"Actually, they didn't give up so easily. They decided to use Daniel's faith to get him in trouble."

"That's not nice! God's children shouldn't get in trouble for serving the Father!" Ariana stomped her little angel foot in anger.

"Unfortunately, life is not always fair. Now, Daniel was very serious about praying to God every day. The other rulers knew this so they tricked the king into signing a new law which said that people could only pray to the king—no one else."

"Well, that is just silly. Why would anyone want to pray to a plain old king. I mean—"

"Ariana, please stop interrupting

so I can tell you about the angel. Thank you. Now Daniel knew about the new law. But, he still went home and knelt down right in front of his open window and prayed to God, three times a day."

"Right in front of the window, why didn't he pray in a closet or under his bed? Ooops, sorry." Michael's glare reminded Ariana she had interrupted again.

"Of course Daniel's enemies were outside his window watching for him to break the law. When he did, they grabbed him and brought him to the king. The punishment for breaking the new law was being thrown into a den of lions. The king did not want to punish Daniel, but the law is the law. He had no choice. The king tried to think of some way to protect Daniel, but there was no way out. He said, 'Daniel, I hope your God will save you.' Then the soldiers threw Daniel into a pit full of hungry lions and put a big rock over the opening."

"Those other rulers thought they had won, didn't they? But, this is where the angel comes in, right? Am I right, Sir?" Ariana was jumping up and down with excitement.

"Yes. You're right," Michael was nearly as excited as Ariana. "The rulers surely thought they had won. The next morning the king hurried to the lions' den. When the big

rock was moved, he expected to see lions with full tummies—and no Daniel. Instead, he heard Daniel's voice! 'O King, my God sent His angel to keep the lions' mouths shut. They didn't even hurt me!' The king was happy—no—he was overjoyed! He took Daniel out of that lions' den in a flash, and he told everyone to fear Daniel's God because He is very powerful."

"Yeaaaaaa! The Father protected Daniel with a brave angel. Yeaaa! All the angel had to do was hold some lions' mouths closed." Ariana was jumping and cheering at the top

of her lungs. "I could do that, Sir. I know I could. I'm going to practice right now. Have you seen any lions around here?"

"Well, Ariana, it might be best to start a bit smaller than a lion. Why don't you practice with your kitten?" Michael suggested. "But be careful not to hurt it."

"Great idea, I'll see you later!" shouted Ariana as she hurried off.

"I am certain you will," Michael sighed. "I am certain you will."

Thinking It Over

• Why were the rulers jealous of Daniel?
• Have you ever been in trouble because you believe in God? What happened?

HIDE–AND–SEEK

EXODUS 13:21-22; 14:19-20

"All-e-all-e-in-free," Ariana shouted as she ran from hiding place to hiding place.

"What does 'all-e-all-e-in-free' mean?" Michael asked as Ariana came back to the home-base tree.

"Oh, my friends and I are playing hide–and–seek. I've been looking for them and I can't find them. Now I want to stop looking so I call 'all-e-all-e-in-free' and they can come out

of their hiding places without being caught." This explanation seemed simple to Ariana, but Michael looked a bit confused.

"You know Ariana, I remember a time when an angel helped the whole nation of Israel play hide-and-seek," he said.

Ariana left her game and followed Michael. "The whole nation? That must have been thousands of people. How did a whole nation play hide-and-seek? Who were they hiding from? You know, if serving the Father means playing a game like hide-and-seek, then I'm ready."

"Sit down, Little One," Michael laughed. "I'll tell you all about it." When she was settled, he began. "Well, you know the story of how the Israelites were slaves in Egypt. They had been slaves for a long time, and they prayed and prayed that God would help them get free."

"Right, and God sent Moses to tell the Pharaoh to let them go, and he said no, and God said yes, and he said no, and…"

"I see you remember the story. Well, as you know Moses finally convinced Pharaoh that God meant business. After the ten terrible things happened to the Egyptians, Pharaoh said the Israelites could leave. So Moses led the Israelites out of Egypt. Just imagine thousands of men, women, and children with all their possessions and all their animals."

"That must have been quite a parade," Ariana said.

"Yes, and the Angel of the Lord led the whole group. In the daytime he was in a big, tall cloud that led them on their way. At night the cloud became fire. The people only had to look up to see that God was with them and was leading them."

"That's a cool story, Mr. Michael.

But I don't see how it has anything to do with hide–and–seek."

"Oh, well, we have to go back to Egypt to find that part of the story. You see, when Pharaoh realized that he had let all his slaves leave, and there was no one to do the work, he changed his mind again. He sent the whole Egyptian army out to bring the Israelites back. The army had chariots and horses, so they quickly caught up to the Israelites."

"That guy had trouble making decisions, didn't he?"

"Only trouble sticking with them. Anyway, when the Israelites saw the

Egyptian army chasing them, they were very scared. They started complaining about Moses bringing them out in the desert to die. They were backed up to the Red Sea so there was no place to get away from the Egyptians. That's when God's angel and the cloud moved around to the back of the Israelites. The cloud got

bigger and bigger. Soon it was so big that the Israelites and the Egyptians couldn't even see each other."

"Hide–and–seek! I bet no one called 'all-e-all-e-in-free'."

"Right. No one did. The Egyptians waited for the cloud to go away and for light to come so they could see the Israelites again. In the meantime, God parted the waters of the Red Sea and the Israelites walked through on dry ground to the other side. When the cloud finally moved, the Egyptians rushed into the sea after the Israelites, but God let the waters come down on them and they were all drowned."

"Wow! I wonder what other games the Father lets angels play with His people? How about Red Rover, Red Rover?"

"Ariana, this angel hide–and–seek was really not a game. It was a matter of life and death for the Israelites."

"Right, right. Let's see, Red Light, Green Light, Simon Says . . . I will think of lots of games, Sir."

"I am certain you will," Michael sighed. "I am certain you will."

Thinking It Over

• Why did God have to hide the Israelites?

•Thank God for a time when He protected you.

A VERY HOT DAY

DANIEL 3:1-29

Ariana watched the flames of the campfire shoot higher and higher. She didn't even hear Michael come up beside her. "Fire is an amazing thing isn't it, Ariana?"

"O, Mr. Michael, Sir, I didn't hear you. Actually, fire kind of scares me. I guess because it's so powerful. I don't want to get too close."

"You know, Ariana, I remember one time when an angel had to walk right into a fire to protect three of the Father's children."

"Really? Was he scared?" Ariana couldn't believe anyone, even an angel, would *want* to walk into a fire.

"He might have been scared. But he knew that God would not ask him to do something without giving His protection. Would you like to hear the story?"

"Oh yes," said Ariana. So Michael sat down next to her. He watched the campfire for a while before beginning.

"Shadrach, Meshach, and Abednego are the three men who needed protection this time. They

were prisoners of King Nebuchadnezzar, and they did something that made the king very angry."

"It's not a good idea to make kings angry," Ariana whispered.

"Right. But this is what happened. King Nebuchadnezzar made a huge golden statue of himself. Then he announced to the whole kingdom, that whenever the people heard music, they should bow down and worship the statue. That was fine for most people. But Shadrach, Meshach, and Abednego loved God.

They would not worship anyone or anything but Him. The punishment for not obeying the king's command was to be thrown into a blazing, hot furnace."

"Didn't they get a warning or anything?" Ariana asked.

"When the king heard about their refusal, he did give them one more chance. But they knew they could not worship anyone except God. In fact, they said, 'We aren't even worried about what will happen to us. You can throw us in the fire, and God will protect us.' "

"They were very brave!"

"Not so much brave as trusting. They knew the Father would take care of them. Anyway, when they refused to worship the king's statue the second time, the king told his workers to heat the furnace up hotter than ever. Then he ordered the three men to be tied up and thrown into the fire. The fire was so hot that the men who threw in Shadrach, Meshach, and Abednego were killed!"

Ariana gulped and scooted back from the campfire a bit. "When does the angel part come in?" she asked.

"I guess it can come in right now. The king sat down and watched the fire. He was sure he had taken care of the three disobedient Jews. But as he looked into the furnace he saw something he could not believe! 'Guards,' he called. 'How many men did you throw into the fire?'

" 'Three, Sir,' was the response.

" 'Then why do I see FOUR men walking around in there—and not even tied up, not even hurt?'"

"Who is the fourth man? Where did he come from? Is he the angel?" Ariana bubbled with questions.

"Yes, Ariana. The fourth man was the angel God sent to protect the three men," Michael answered.

"I bet the king wasn't too happy about this, was he?" Ariana asked.

"No. He wasn't. He went to the door of the furnace and called: 'Shadrach, Meshach, Abednego, come out here!' When they came out, everyone crowded around to see them. They were not burned at all. *They didn't even smell like smoke!*

"Nebuchadnezzar was impressed with the God of Israel. He said, 'Praise the God of Shadrach, Meshach, and Abednego! He sent an angel to protect them because they will worship none but Him!'"

The campfire had burned down to embers and the night air was chilly. Ariana didn't say anything for

a while. She just stared at the dying fire. Finally she spoke softly, "Mr. Michael, Sir. Maybe I won't ever be used in the Father's service. I don't think I could ever go into a fire."

"Ariana, don't be discouraged. You may never be asked to go into a fire. Every angel has a specialty. Some can go into fires, some can be invisible, some make announcements. We all have our specialties. You just haven't found yours yet, that's all. Now, it's getting cold out here. You'd

better go inside."

"Yes, Sir. Oh, and Mr. Michael, I'm going to keep looking for my speciality. I'll come talk to you some more tomorrow," she said as she ran toward home.

"I am certain you will," Michael said. "I am certain you will."

Thinking It Over

• Why were Shadrach, Meshach, and Abednego thrown into the furnace?
• Thank God for being with you when you follow Him and others around you don't.

RUN FOR YOUR LIFE

GENESIS 19:1-25

Michael was tossing a ball high in the air and watching his new puppy chase it. Goldy trotted back to Michael for another toss. But he was interrupted just as he was ready to throw it. "Mr. Michael, Sir," Ariana seemed to appear out of thin air. Michael thought perhaps she had learned to make herself invisible after all. "Mr. Michael, I have a question."

"I will be happy to answer it if I can," Michael said, tossing the ball for Goldy.

"God's children sometimes get themselves in some bad trouble, don't they? I mean like Peter in prison and Daniel in the lions' den. So I was wondering, why doesn't the Father help them BEFORE they get in trouble?"

"Sometimes He does. But often He wants to show them and the people around them how powerful He is by how He saves them. Remember how the king in the story of Daniel praised God after Daniel was saved?"

"Yes. I remember. But could I hear a story of when He helped before the trouble started. Did He ask an angel to help?" Ariana asked.

"Certainly, let me tell you the story of Lot and the angel who helped him," Michael said. He sat down and lifted Goldy up on his lap. "Lot and his family lived in the city of Sodom. It was a terrible place, full of evil people who did not love God."

"Why would any of God's people want to live in a place like that?" Ariana was truly puzzled.

"That is a whole other story. Right now let me tell you how the Father got Lot and his family out of that city. They had to get out fast because God decided to destroy the whole city because of all the wicked people there. He was going to rain down fire on it."

"Oh no, not fire!" Ariana fell back on the floor. Fire was one thing that really frightened the little angel.

"It's all right, Little One. They got out before the fire came. But Lot was not just going to leave Sodom without some pushing. So the Father sent two angels. Their job was to tell Lot that he *had* to get out of the city. They did tell him, but he didn't listen right away. He talked to his sons-in-law and they didn't see any reason to hurry. So Lot didn't either."

"Wait a minute, I thought you said the Father helped *before* the trouble started," Ariana said suspicious.

"He did. Just listen. Anyway, the next morning the angels told Lot again that he had to get out of the city. Believe it or not, Lot still did not leave right away."

"Does this guy have to be hit with a brick, or what?"

"Ariana, please do not talk like that! Where was I? Oh, yes, the angels actually grabbed Lot and his wife and daughters by the hands and pulled them out of the city. 'Run for your lives. And don't look back. Go up into the mountains. You have to get out of here, or you will die!' the angels shouted.

"But Lot said, 'Oh, please don't make us go to the mountains, can't we go to that little town over there?'"

"Ugh, Lot never learns, does he?" Ariana wasn't sure she would have liked this one of God's children.

"The angels agreed to Lot's request. And just as he and his family reached the little town, fire fell from the sky and burned up Sodom. They made it out just in time!"

"Well, I guess the Father did save Lot before the real trouble began. But there wasn't much time to spare, was there?" Ariana lay back and looked up at the clouds floating by. She did not say anything for quite a while. "The Father really loves His children, doesn't He? He tries so hard to protect them. The work that we angels do to help is very important, isn't it?"

"That's what I've been trying to teach you, Little One. You have been learning from these stories, after all," Michael said.

124

"Yes and someday I'm going to be the best angel in the angel brigade!" Ariana saluted Michael and marched away.

"I am certain you will, Little One," Michael said softly. "I am certain you will."

Thinking It Over

• Why did Lot have to get out of Sodom?

• Ask a grown-up to tell you about a time God protected him or her.

Comfort

FOOD SERVICE

1 KINGS 19:5-11

"MR. MICHAEL, SIR!" Ariana burst into Michael's office with such force that every book on the top of his bookshelf tumbled to the floor. "Oops. Sorry," she said, picking up the books.

"Just stack them by the desk," Michael said. "Did you want to talk to me about something?"

"Yes, Sir. I just figured out that the last few stories you've told me

127

about angel work have been about *protecting* the children. They all kind of scared me, so maybe protecting isn't my specialty. I mean, I am kind of little to be protecting grown-ups. You have told me about announcements, and I'm sure I could do that. And you told me about instructing, but I may be too small for that. Are there any other jobs the Father asks us to do?"

"Wise observation, Little One," Michael smiled. "Yes. There are other jobs. Let me think…another job is *comforting*. Sometimes we have comforted God's children, and sometimes we have comforted Jesus the Son Himself."

"I can do that, I can! I'm very, very comfortable!" Ariana cried. She was bouncing all around Michael's desk.

Michael smiled. "Well, let me think of an example. Then you can see how this comforting job sounds. Oh, I know a good example. The story of Elijah. He was one of God's children who was discouraged. He definitely needed comforting. Elijah had made a very powerful king and queen mad at him. He had to run for his life. He walked for a whole day into the desert. All by himself."

"Poor Elijah! I don't like to be by myself. It makes me lonely. He should have asked the Father to get that king and…"

"SShhh, Little One. You know that isn't the way the Father works. Anyway, now Elijah was all alone in the desert. He was very discouraged. He said, 'Lord, why don't You just let me die?' Then he lay

down and fell asleep."

"That's good. He was probably just tired. A good nap can work wonders. But Mr. Michael, you didn't mention an angel or comforting."

"I'm not finished, Ariana. The Father knew that Elijah needed some sleep. He also knew that after resting, Elijah needed to eat to get his strength back. So, the Father sent an angel with food and water for Elijah."

"Food? You mean to be a comforting angel I have to be able to cook? I'm little. I can't even reach the oven controls." Ariana was totally frustrated.

Michael ignored her outburst and continued his story. "Elijah ate and then went back to sleep. Later, the

Father sent the angel back again with more food. He told Elijah to get up and eat because he had a long journey ahead. Elijah obeyed and he was ready for the journey when the time came. So what do you think?"

"I have a question. Did the angel get to have some of the food?" Ariana asked with a twinkle in her eye. Before Michael could answer she said, "I think I could do a comforting job if I didn't have to be invisible, or

go through locked doors, or go in fire. OK, I'll take a comforting job."

"I am certain you will," Michael said. "I am certain you will."

Thinking It Over

• How was Elijah comforted?
• When have you needed God's comfort?

GOOD NEWS

MATTHEW 28:2-8

Michael settled down at the library table. He was soon deep in thought as he studed the Scriptures. But his study time didn't last long, "Mr. Michael Sir, I brought your lunch. I baked fresh bread all by myself, uhhh—almost. You'll feel so-o-o-o good after you eat," Ariana sang the words.

"Ariana, it isn't lunch time. Why are you bringing me food?" Michael whispered.

"'Cause that's what a comforting angel does. See Mr. Michael, I can be a comforting angel," Ariana was very proud of herself.

"Well, thank you for lunch. I'll have it in a few hours—when it is lunch time. But you know, bringing food is not the only job of a comforter angel. Let's go outside and I'll tell you a story that shows a different part of the job," Michael said.

When they settled on a park bench, Ariana opened the bag and broke off a piece of bread for herself. Michael did not even notice as he started the story. "Right after Jesus died was a very unhappy time for His followers. They were sad and confused. Early one morning, a few days after Jesus was buried, two women went to His tomb. As they got near it, there was a strong earthquake. Everything rocked and shook, but the most amazing thing was that the big, heavy stone in front of the opening to the tomb rolled away."

Ariana's big eyes grew even bigger. "Did the comforter angel move it?" she asked.

"Yes. He did. The Father had a special message for those two women. It would make them feel better about all that had happened to Jesus. So as the earth shook, the angel rolled the big stone away. Then he sat down on top of it."

"Well, sure, he was probably tired. Moving a stone as big as that one would be hard work!"

"When the women looked up at the stone," Michael continued, "they saw something they could hardly believe. There sat an angel, but he did not look like you and I look right now. His face was as bright as lightning and his clothing was so white it hurt to look at him!"

"Oh my, that sounds scary. Were the women afraid?"

"It was scary. In fact the two soldiers guarding the tomb fell down as if they were dead. But the angel turned to the women right away and said, 'Don't be afraid!' Then he gave them the message that would make them feel better than anything. He said, 'I know you are here looking for Jesus. He isn't here. He has come

back to life, just as He said He would.'"

"Yippee! Weren't they excited? Didn't they jump up and down and cheer?" Ariana certainly was.

"Yes, Little One. They were excited, afraid, happy, all at once. The angel told them to go tell the rest of Jesus' friends that He was alive. So they ran to town."

"I gotta go, Mr. Michael. Here's your lunch," Ariana started to dash away.

"Ariana, where is my fresh-baked bread?" Michael asked.

"Um, I guess I was nibbling on it a little bit while you told that wonderfully exciting story. I really gotta go, Sir."

"What's your hurry?"

"I'm going to lift weights. If I

have to move big stones, I need bigger muscles! I'll be back, Mr. Michael!" she called over her shoulder.

"I am certain you will," said Michael. "I am certain you will."

Thinking It Over

• What was the angel's message to the women?
• Thank God that Jesus came back to life.

A SAD MOTHER

GENESIS 21:1-20

Michael enjoyed working in his garden. He liked the feel of the soft earth and putting the small plants in the soil. Today he was weeding the plants, humming softly as he worked. But the peacefulness was soon disrupted.

"Look, Mr. Michael. Look at my muscles," Ariana shouted over the fence, bending her arms to show her muscles.

"Very impressive, Ariana," Michael said. The little angel was quite proud of the pea-sized bumps on her arm.

"So, have you got a comforting job I can do for the Father? I can move big stones now. You can trust me, Mr. Michael. I'll do a good job!" Ariana kept flexing her muscles as she talked.

"Actually, very few comforting jobs require big muscles. More often a comforter needs a kind and sensitive heart."

"I have that. Well, most of the time I do. Sometimes. ..." Ariana knew she was on thin ice here. Sometimes she did not sound very sensitive or kind.

"Come over here and I'll tell you about when an angel had to deliver God's message to Hagar. He had to be gentle and kind. Hagar was very sad."

Ariana hurried to the gate. Soon she was sitting beside Michael. "May I hear that story?" Ariana asked.

Michael brushed the dirt from his hands before beginning. "Hagar was the maid of Abraham's wife, Sarah. Now the unusual thing about Hagar was that she had a son, Ishmael, and the father of the boy was Abraham. This was something that Sarah had arranged before she and Abraham had been able to have a baby. That's a story for another day," Michael said when he saw Ariana glance up with a questioning look on her face.

"Of course, you know that Abraham and Sarah had a son, too. His name was Isaac. Things were going fine until one day when Sarah saw Ishmael teasing Isaac. She became very angry and insisted that Abraham get rid of Hagar and Ishmael. So early the next morning, Abraham gave Hagar and Ishmael some food and water and sent them away."

"Was that hard for him?" Ariana asked softly.

"Yes. It was hard. But God told him not to worry. He said He would make Ishmael into a great nation."

Ariana stood up. "Well, that's a happy ending. But I didn't hear about any angel work."

"I'm not finished. Hagar and Ishmael hiked deep into the wilderness. Before long their food and water ran out. Ishmael started crying and Hagar was very sad. She didn't know what to do. Finally, she just put Ishmael down beside a tree and she walked off a little way from him. She was sure he was going to die and she didn't

want to watch. Hagar sat down and started to cry herself. She sobbed and sobbed."

"Poor Hagar. What a scary time! Now is when the angel helps, right?"

"That's right. The angel came to her and gently asked, 'What's wrong Hagar? You don't have to be afraid. God has heard Ishmael crying. He is going to take care of your son. Pick him up and hold him. God will make a great nation from Ishmael.' Then God showed Hagar a well. She got water for Ishmael and herself, and they both felt much better."

"Well, that was a pretty easy angel job. I could even do that one." Ariana was pretty smug.

"Gentle, Ariana, gentle. Didn't you hear the gentleness with which the angel spoke to Hagar. The Father told him how sad and worried Hagar was. He had to be very gentle."

"Gentle, right. Got it. I'm going to go practice gentle. I'll be back later to show you how gentle I am," Ariana said softly.

"I am certain you will," Michael said. "I am certain you will."

Thinking It Over

• Why was Hagar crying?
• Look up 1 Peter 5:7. What does this verse tell you about the times when you are worried or sad?

144

RESISTING TEMPTATION

MATTHEW 4:1-11

"**I**'m depressed," Ariana mumbled. She plopped down on Michael's office floor, shoulders sagging and head drooping.

"Why are you depressed?" Michael asked.

"Well, I was thinking about all the stories you have told me lately about how we angels help the Father. I was beginning to think we are pretty important. But then, I remembered that God's children don't need us. They have the Father, who can do anything to look out for them; they have the Holy Spirit whom the Father sent to live with them after Jesus went back to heaven. They even have Jesus who helps them, too. When it comes right down to it, we aren't very important."

"Ariana, we don't do our work so we will be important. We do it to serve and help the Father in any way we can. Of course, He could get the work done without us, but we are

grateful He chooses to use our help sometimes. Maybe it would help you to hear how some angels once helped Jesus."

"Well, I know an angel told Joseph to take the baby to Egypt so He would be safe," Ariana wasn't really interested in more stories.

"Yes, but there were a few other times, after Jesus was grown up, when we were asked to help Him."

"It would be quite an honor to help Jesus. I mean, He is the heart of God's whole plan, isn't He? OK, tell me one more story," she said, lying back on the floor.

"Well, one time the Father asked for angel help was when Satan took Jesus out to the desert. The devil was going to tempt Him and try to get Him to turn from God and serve the devil. For forty whole days and nights, Jesus didn't eat anything. Satan knew He was hungry, so he came and said, 'If you are the Son of God, turn these rocks into bread.'"

"Forty days and nights with no food?" Ariana couldn't believe it. "He must have been very hungry. But He didn't do what Satan said, did He?"

"No, He didn't. He told Satan that

there were more important things in the world than food. Then Satan took Him up to the highest part of the temple in Jerusalem. He said, 'Jump down, Jesus. If You are the Son of God, angels will be there to catch You so You won't be hurt.' "

"He got that right. We would be there, wouldn't we, Mr. Michael? We wouldn't let God's Son get hurt!"

"Shhh. Let me finish. Jesus told Satan that he shouldn't try to test God. Then Satan took Him to a high mountain and showed Him all the kingdoms in the world. He said, 'Jesus, I will give all this to You if You will bow down and worship me.' "

"Boy, he doesn't give up, does he?"

"Jesus said, 'Get away from Me Satan. The Scriptures say to worship God and only serve Him!' Then Satan left."

"Jesus must have been pretty tired out after all that tempting. Especially when He hadn't eaten for forty days!" Ariana was stuck on that point.

"Yes, He was tired out. So, the Father sent some angels to help Him."

"How did they help? What did they do?"

"They did whatever He needed. Some brought food and water, some helped Him rest, some encouraged Him. We were there for whatever Jesus needed."

"Cool story Mr. M, uhhh, Michael. I guess I can see that the work we do is important after all. But when am I going to get a chance to serve?"

"I am certain you will, Ariana," Michael encouraged. "I am certain you will."

Thinking It Over

• When have you been tempted to do something wrong?
• What can you learn from Jesus' example?

ARIANA'S TURN

REVELATION 7:11-13

Michael was carefully studying the paper in his hand as he hurried out of his office. But his concentration was quickly broken when he tripped and sprawled on the floor. "Oh, Mr. Michael, I'm so sorry. Are you OK?" Ariana asked as she helped him up.

"What happened?" Michael asked himself, as much as Ariana.

"I was just sitting here on the floor by your office door," Ariana began. "You came out so quickly that

151

I didn't have time to move. I guess you sort of tripped over my legs."

"Why were you sitting outside my office?" Michael's steady patience was being tested.

"Mr. Michael, every time the Father asks an angel to help with His work, I hurry to your office to volunteer. But every time someone else is chosen. I thought if I just stayed here, you might think of me first next time."

Michael sighed a long sigh. "Ariana, I know how eager you are to serve the Father. You have listened patiently to all my stories, explaining how we angels serve Him."

"Yes and I learned how to shine and how to be

invisible and how to be gentle and how to give announcements. Mr. Michael, I tried to learn everything you said was important. What else can I do?" Ariana cried.

"I'm afraid that all you can do is wait for your time," Michael said kindly.

Ariana looked at him with big sad eyes, "I wish I could serve the Father now."

Just then Michael had an idea. "Ariana, I have an errand to do, but can you meet me back here in a couple of hours?"

"I guess so, but why?"

"Just meet me here. And wear a clean robe."

That is why Ariana was standing at Michael's office door now. Dressed up in a clean robe, her hair freshly combed, she knew something important was about to happen to her. Suddenly Michael's door opened and he came striding out. Without saying a word, he took Ariana by the hand and started down a long hallway with a very high ceiling. The walls were lined with mirrors. Ariana was full of questions, but she knew this was not the time to ask them.

Michael stopped in front of two enormous doors. Then he turned and smiled gently at her. "Ariana, I would like to invite you to join your fellow angels in one of our most wonderful opportunities to serve the Father."

Slowly the big doors opened. Ariana hesitantly walked into the room. It was full of angels. *I didn't even know there were so many angels,* she thought. Everyone was standing around a beautiful, golden throne. Ariana edged around the crowd to see who was sitting in it. Her breath caught in her throat when she saw...it was *the Lord, God*! Suddenly all the angels fell to the floor saying, "Praise and glory, wisdom and thanks, honor and power and strength be to our God forever and ever." Ariana's heart overflowed with respect and honor and love as she joined the

other angels in praising God.

Michael knelt beside Ariana and slipped his arm around the little angel's shoulder. She looked up at him and smiled the most angelic smile he had ever seen. Then the two friends turned to the throne and together praised God the Father.

Thinking It Over

Dear God,
Thank You that Ariana found a way she could serve You. Thank You that You accept praise from any of Your children, no matter how young or old. Amen.

A Word about Angels

As children read and hear biblical
accounts about angels, they may
ask, "What do angels really look
like?" Illustrators through the
ages have drawn their ideas, but
the Bible gives only a few details.
What is most important about
angels is the comforting reality of
their existence and their ability to
minister to all who love God.

Parents—

Are you looking for fun ways to bring the Bible to life in the lives of your children?

Chariot Family publishing has hundreds of books, toys, games, and videos that help you teach your children the Bible and apply it to their everyday lives. Look for these educational, inspirational, and fun products at your local Christian bookstore.

For more about angels, look for

Ariana, the Little Angel
All girls would be just thrilled to have their own little angel—and now they can with "Ariana, the Little Angel" doll available from Rainfall. This beautiful soft and fully dressable doll will help teach children more about angels.

"Ariana, the Little Angel" doll is a perfect play-along companion to *The Little Angel's Bible Stories book.*

Interest level: Ages 3 and up
SPCN: 612-598-561X

A Child's Book of Angels
Bible stories featuring angels in action answer questions children have about angels.

Interest level: Ages 3–8
ISBN 1-55513-756-3

Angels, Angels All Around
Twelve stories of angels, retold with a spirit of whimsy and drama.

Interest level: Ages 9–12
ISBN 0-7459-2623-1